BRITISH HERITAGE

The
ANGLO-SAXONS

Robert Hull

British Heritage

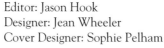

The Anglo-Saxons
The Celts in Britain
The Romans in Britain
The Tudors
The Victorians
The Vikings in Britain

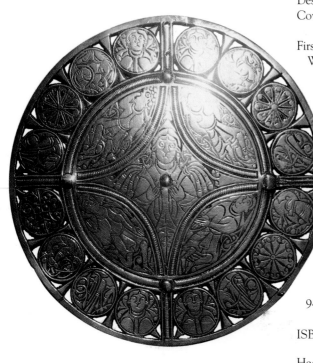

Editor: Jason Hook
Designer: Jean Wheeler
Cover Designer: Sophie Pelham

First published in 1997 by
Wayland Publishers,

This edition published in 2007 by Wayland,
an imprint of Hachette Children's Books

British Library Cataloguing in Publication Data
Hull, Robert
The Anglo-Saxons. - (Heritages)
1. Anglo-Saxons - England - Juvenile literature
2. Great Britain - History - Anglo-Saxon period, 449-
1066 - Juvenile literature
3. England - Civilization - To 1066 - Juvenile literature
I.Title
942'.01

ISBN 978 0 7502 5211 9

Hachette Children's Books
338 Euston Road, London NW1 3BH

Printed and bound in China

Contents

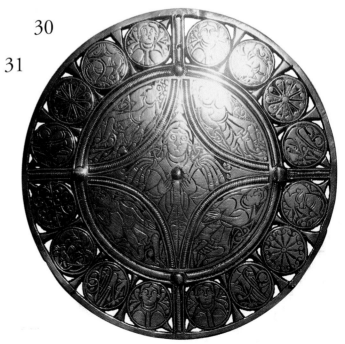

chapter one

WHO WERE THE ANGLO-SAXONS?

The Anglo-Saxons – the people who became the English – left many things behind them; things we can see, touch, marvel at and study. They left the dark shadows of their villages on our hillsides; city walls and churches that still stand; richly filled graves, and coins that are still found in fields. They left us swords, letters, fabulous jewels, place-names, paintings, poems, beautiful books, and legends like those about King Arthur. They left us English, our language.

▲ *Fragments of this helmet were found in an Anglo-Saxon grave at Sutton Hoo.*

▼ *A map showing the Anglo-Saxon movement to Britain in the fifth century.*

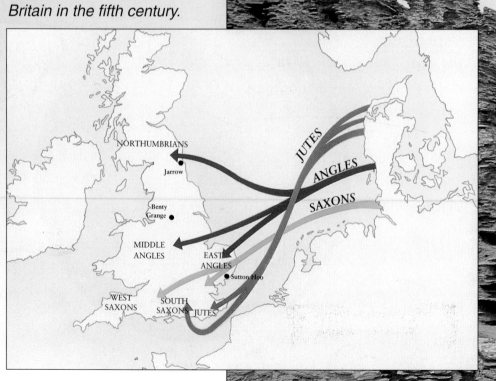

NORTHUMBRIANS

Jarrow

Benty
Grange

MIDDLE
ANGLES

EAST
ANGLES

Sutton Hoo

WEST
SAXONS

SOUTH
SAXONS   JUTES

JUTES

ANGLES

SAXONS

4

The Anglo-Saxons came from various European tribes – Angles, Saxons, Jutes, Franks and Frisians. They lived in the south of what is now Denmark, and along the sandy coast of north-west Germany and Holland.

A group of these tribes came to Britain around AD 420, to help defend the British against the Picts. Twenty years later, they rebelled and began fighting the British. A bitter war went on for about fifty years. The Anglo-Saxons, or 'English' as they called themselves, gradually settled down on land surrounded by the British.

By the middle of the fifth century many Anglo-Saxons had rowed across the North Sea to Britain, to settle there. Some were farmers seeking better land for their crops. Some came because the North Sea had started to rise, and they believed that their villages would be flooded.

During the fifth century, Britain changed in many ways. Features of the Roman occupation of Britain – baths, theatres, large houses with underfloor heating and mosaics – gradually became things of the past.

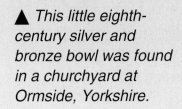

▲ *This little eighth-century silver and bronze bowl was found in a churchyard at Ormside, Yorkshire.*

◄ *According to legend, this ruin at Tintagel in Cornwall was the birthplace of King Arthur, who some believe fought the Anglo-Saxons in the sixth century.*

5

chapter two

WHEN DID THE ANGLO-SAXONS COME TO BRITAIN?

Before 600 the only British book about the Anglo-Saxons' arrival was written in Latin by a monk called Gildas. Gildas was furious with the British kings. 'They were struck blind,' he wrote. 'To hold back the northern peoples, they introduced into the island the vile unspeakable Saxons.'

Roman control of Britain grew weaker during the fourth century. The Romans had trouble in other parts of their empire and started to withdraw troops from Britain. In 410, the Roman Emperor wrote a letter giving the British people permission to carry arms. In other words, the Britons must now learn to defend themselves.

Britons led by their king, Vortigern, appealed to Europe for help against the invading Picts: 'Vortigern invited the Angles hither, and they came to Britain in three ships at a place called Ebbsfleet. King Vortigern gave them land ... on condition they fought against the Picts.' The Anglo-Saxons beat the Picts back, and gave instructions for their comrades back home 'to be told of the worthlessness of the Britons and the excellence of the land'.

We know things like these, because we still have Anglo-Saxon histories. A lot of our information comes from the *Anglo-Saxon Chronicle*, which was written during the reign of King Alfred.

◄ *A page from the* Anglo-Saxon Chronicle. *At the top is the Latin word 'cometa', meaning comet. Comets were recorded as omens of future events.*

The *Chronicle* tells us that in 455 the Anglo-Saxons rebelled. The Britons 'forsook Kent and fled to London in great terror'. The Anglo-Saxons 'slew many Welsh'. The Anglo-Saxon word *wealas* means both foreigners and slaves. To the Saxon invaders, all Britons were *wealas*. We get the word 'Welsh' from it.

A famous writer called The Venerable Bede says in his book, *A History of the English Church and People,* that the Britons fought back: 'Ambrosius Aurelianus, their leader, with God's help inflicted a great defeat on the invaders.'

After Ambrosius died, the war was carried on for about twenty years, perhaps under the legendary King Arthur. Some writers believe that Arthur never existed. Others believe that he was responsible for the Britons' great victory over the English at Badon Hill.

An eighth century writer, Nennius, says: 'At Badon Hill, 960 men perished at one charge.' He writes that the Britons were led by Arthur. He also says that Arthur slaughtered all 960!

▼ *Legends link King Arthur's court at Camelot with this Iron Age hill-fort at Cadbury, Somerset. Lines of defence added there in AD 500 can still be seen.*

chapter three

WHICH PARTS OF BRITAIN DID THE ENGLISH CONQUER?

▼ *A pathway still follows Offa's Dyke, which once stretched from sea to sea for 240 kilometres. (Inset) A map of the seven kingdoms founded by the Jutes (orange), Angles (red) and Saxons (green), who became the English.*

The English now began to conquer. The *Chronicle* is full of the dates of their victorious battles. They defeated several British kings, and set up their own independent kingdoms. In 585, the English founded Mercia. To the north, after the defeat of a British army at Catterick, the English kingdom of Northumbria stretched from coast to coast.

Eastern Britain was turning into England. The names of some Anglo-Saxon kingdoms, like Northumbria and East Anglia, are still used; but we have forgotten the smaller kingdoms, such as Deira and Elmet.

SCOTS AND PICTS

LINDISFARNE

Jarrow

NORTHUMBRIA

Offa's Dyke

M E R C I A

EAST ANGLIA

WELSH

Sutton Hoo

ESSEX

Cadbury

KENT

Tintagel

W E S S E X

SUSSEX

Canterbury

Hastings

Wareham

This violence slowly calmed down. Kings were converted to Christianity, and many soldiers became monks. There was less opportunity for fighting when only a few large kingdoms remained. The big fish like Mercia and Northumbria had eaten all the little fish like Hwicce, in the Gloucestershire area, and Lyndsey, south of Lincoln.

But the British – who became the Welsh, Scots, and Cornish – were always hostile to the Anglo-Saxon kings on their borders. In the eighth century, King Offa of Mercia built Offa's Dyke – a turf wall 3 m high and 9 m wide with a ditch and a stone top, to keep the Welsh out of what was now England. Its construction employed thousands of men. Mercia must have been a highly organized kingdom to achieve such a feat of engineering.

One mystery of these times is what happened to the British in the new English kingdoms. No writing or objects left in the earth can tell us clearly. Many stayed on, especially where there were only a few English. Some may have carried on farming in remote hills, or disappeared into slavery.

Others moved west, to settle alongside Britons in Wales, Cornwall, Devon or even Ireland. Many left to settle in north-west Spain; and in Brittany, which takes its name from the Britons.

▼ *This Anglo-Saxon sword was found in Yorkshire. According to legend, Offa carved the route of his dyke with his sword-point.*

Offa was well-known in Europe. In a letter to him, Emperor Charlemagne of the Holy Roman Empire asks Offa to send more cloaks, and promises in return to send the 'black stones' – probably grindstones – which Offa had asked for.

9

The Vikings and Alfred

After a few generations of English had begun to feel that England was their country, the Vikings attacked. The age of the Anglo-Saxons became the age of the Vikings too.

England was saved for the Anglo-Saxons by the King of Wessex, Alfred. The Vikings began raiding late in the eighth century. A Welsh monk called Asser, who wrote the story of Alfred's life, describes how Alfred had to shelter in the Somerset marshes while building up an army to face the Vikings.

Alfred defeated the Danish Viking Guthrum in 878, after years of fighting, and the Danes and the Anglo-Saxons divided England between them. The Danish part was called the Danelaw.

▲ *The boar on this helmet from Benty Grange, Derbyshire, recalls the warriors in the Anglo-Saxon poem* Beowulf: *'Figures of boars, gold-adorned, shining ... glittered over their cheek-pieces. The warlike beast guarded the lives of the fierce warriors.'*

▶ *The shape of the earth walls raised round the burh town of Wareham in Dorset can still be seen.*

English Unity

According to Asser, 'All the Angles and Saxons turned willingly to Alfred and submitted themselves to his lordship.' Alfred prepared to win back the Danish conquests. He raised strong walls round many towns and built twenty-nine fortified towns called *burhs*. Remains of burh walls can still be seen in towns such as Wareham and Wallingford.

Alfred built up an English navy of bigger ships. He also arranged that only half the peasants should be called up to fight, leaving half at home looking after the land. In one earlier battle the peasants had left halfway through to take in the harvest!

The English fought each other too. The *Anglo-Saxon Chronicle* for 626 says: 'Eomaer came from Cwichelm, king of the West Saxons, intending to stab King Edwin, king of Kent.' He failed, and Edwin 'went into Wessex with an army and destroyed five kings'. It was like gang-warfare.

Alfred's son Edward won back Mercia from the Danes; then his grandson Aethelstan recovered Northumbria. Edgar, who ruled until 975, became king of the first united England.

For a while, England was at peace with the Vikings. It was a single state, with an organized government, its own coinage, busy towns and trade, and a strong Church.

▲ *This gold buckle was found at Sutton Hoo. The design of biting beasts, jabbing birds and swirling snakes shows the Viking influence on Anglo-Saxon crafts.*

chapter four

WHAT DO WE KNOW OF ANGLO-SAXON SOCIETY?

In Anglo-Saxon England there were four main social classes. There were kings at the top, nobles (thanes), peasants (churls) and, at the bottom, slaves.

Kings were supreme. Everything depended on their power and influence. The early kings were called 'guardians of treasure, givers of gold'.

▲ A winged fire-dragon from a shield buried at Sutton Hoo.

One of the best-known stories left to us by the Anglo-Saxons is the long poem called *Beowulf*. It was written down about AD 1000 and only one original copy exists. The story is set in Denmark and Sweden, and is about a monster called Grendel who raids the palace of King Hrothgar to eat his soldiers.

Beowulf is the hero who helps Hrothgar by fighting Grendel, Grendel's mother and a fire-dragon. He dies in battle, but saves Hrothgar.

An entire wooden ship was buried in an Anglo-Saxon grave at Sutton Hoo. When it was excavated one thousand years later, the wood had rotted away but the shape remained clear in the outline of the rivets.

◀ This silver and gold bird, inlaid with jewels, adorned a warrior's shield.

The burial goods described in the *Beowulf* ship-burial match perfectly the articles unearthed at Sutton Hoo: 'A mound of treasures from far countries was fetched on board her ... weapons of a warrior, war-gear ... treasures and trappings.'

The *Beowulf* story seems to describe real life. It tells of King Scyld's burial at sea in a flaming ship. The ship unearthed at Sutton Hoo in 1939 was probably the grave of Raedwald, a real king.

In *Beowulf*, King Hrothgar is described as 'the best of those who gave gold'. To keep giving the gold that kept men loyal, a king needed to keep getting it – from someone else. Anglo-Saxon England was full of gold-lust, throne-grabbing, vicious feuding, and violent death. Kings were often murdered or made slaves. When Oswald, king of Northumbria, died in battle in 642, his head and hands were displayed on stakes.

▲ The 'biting beasts' on this Anglo-Saxon purse-lid from Sutton Hoo were also a popular design with the Vikings.

When later kings became Christian, all this changed. In the eleventh century, Archbishop Wulfstan of York wrote that a king 'should govern his people justly ... and be a good shepherd of his flock'. Kings were now consecrated, as monarchs still are.

◀ Fabulous treasures from France, Turkey and Afghanistan found at Sutton Hoo included silverware like christening spoons and this magnificent dish.

Thanes, churls and slaves

Thanes were the wealthy followers of the king, free to travel the country visiting their scattered estates. They had to be ready to fight for the king, and had other duties such as repairing fortresses and bridges. Thanes often had great wealth and owned huge areas of land.

Churls also owned land, but were expected to perform various duties for their lord. They had to work a certain number of days for him, and supply him with produce such as honey, malt and yarn. The churl could own up to five *hides*. A hide – a measurement used for centuries – was the amount of land one family could live on.

In Anglo-Saxon England the lowest social class were the slaves. Slaves were pieces of property, without rights. They were bought and sold like cattle, and inherited with estates. Slaves could be freed for prices varying from sixty pence to twelve sheep.

One eleventh-century estate on the River Severn had these rules: 'At every weir every alternate fish belongs to the lord of the manor, and every rare fish which is of value – sturgeon or porpoise, or sea-fish.'

▲ *This silver buckle decorated with delicately woven threads of gold was made in the seventh century. It shows the wealth of the English and the skill of their smiths.*

◀ *This illustration from an Anglo-Saxon manuscript shows a man flying a hawk. In the* Colloquy *the fowler describes using a hawk as a method for catching wild birds.*

Labour

A little book called the *Colloquy*, written in Wessex in King Alfred's time to give students practice in speaking Latin, gives a fascinating picture of people at work. The shepherd says that he needs dogs to guard his flock against wolves. He also describes how he makes cheese and butter. The fowler says: 'I trick the birds – with nets, with lime, with whistling, with a hawk, with traps.'

The fisherman prefers 'to go to the river with his boat than to go with many boats whale-hunting ... It is a perilous thing to catch a whale'. The ploughman describes his labour then says: 'Mighty hard work it is, for I am not free.' The cobbler cures skins, and from them makes slippers, bottles, reins, purses and other objects, which can all still be seen in museums.

At the end of the book the workers argue about who is most important. They agree that they are all necessary to each other, to form a society.

The merchant's words in the *Colloquy* suggest England was wealthy in Alfred's time: 'I go abroad ... and bring precious things which are not produced in this country ... brocade, silk, gems and gold, dyes, wine and oil, ivory, copper and tin, sulphur and glass ...'

chapter five

WHAT DO WE KNOW OF
ANGLO-SAXON LIFE?

Important clues to how the Anglo-Saxons lived can be found in their laws. After about 600, Anglo-Saxon laws were written down. Most kingdoms had laws that covered every part of society.

After the introduction of Christianity, there were religious laws that showed a fear of pagan magic: 'If anyone is a sender of a storm, in other words a sorcerer, he is to do penance for seven years, three on bread and water.'

Some laws were meant to keep people 'in their place'. The laws of King Ine of Wessex, recorded about 690, punish a man who 'departs from his lord without permission and steals into another shire' with a fine of sixty shillings. There were laws for compensation just as we have today. Under Alfred a *bot* – compensation – of ten shillings was made for a broken rib 'in the skin'. It cost another 5 shillings 'if the skin be broken, and the rib taken out'.

There were even laws about clean and unclean food. Archbishop Ecbert's *Ancient Laws* say: 'If a hen eat human blood, it is lawful to eat it after three months ... If anyone eat anything from which a dog or a mouse has eaten ... he is to sing 100 psalms if he did it consciously, fifty if he did it unconsciously.'

The laws show that women and men had different rights. In divorce, a woman could take half the family's property if she also had to look after the children. If their father died, she was given money and animals to keep, and her male relatives had to look after the family until the children grew up.

This church at Sompting, Sussex has the only surviving Anglo-Saxon spire. Christianity brought with it many new Anglo-Saxon laws.

Wergild

One of the most important Anglo-Saxon customs was the *wergild*. This was money paid to a family in compensation when someone was killed. It helped to prevent the repeated acts of revenge between families known as 'blood-feuds'. The amount of wergild paid depended on the rank of the person killed.

These gold coins were found at Sutton Hoo. Their date suggests that the king was buried after 625. Could they have been used as wergild?

Under King Alfred's laws anyone stealing from a church might have a hand cut off. But this would not happen if the thief paid a wergild. Wergild became a fine, with the amount depending not just on what you did, but on who you were and who you did it to.

Our idea of justice is different. 'Equality before the law' means that it shouldn't matter who an offender is. A Chief Constable caught for speeding should be punished in exactly the same way as others are.

Towns and Trade

Anglo-Saxon kingdoms had towns with organized trade and industry. The trading town of Hamwic, on the River Itchen near Southampton, had streets laid out in a grid pattern. Archaeologists have found that some of the roads were gravelled – perhaps a sign of wealth. Hundreds of animal bones have been dug up, suggesting that Hamwic sent animal skins for export.

Anglo-Saxon workshops created some of the most beautiful jewellery and metalwork ever made. Precious swords, pins, rings and brooches of gold and silver show the spectacular skill of English smiths. Some of this wealth belonged to the Church. Some was buried in hoards, hidden away in times of danger. Other objects have been found in graves.

▼ This brooch, called the Fuller Brooch, shows the five senses, with sight in the centre surrounded by smell, touch, hearing and taste.

Many villages had a smithy where tools were made for the farm. In the village of Mucking, in Essex, archaeologists have found signs of Anglo-Saxon weaving. Women were responsible for both spinning and weaving. Many also did embroidery, a beautiful example of which was found in the coffin of St Cuthbert, in Durham Cathedral.

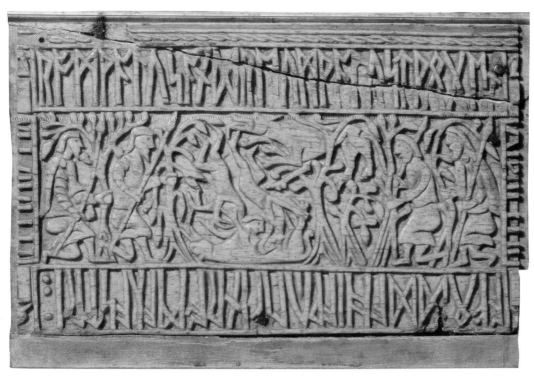

◄ *This casket was carved from whale-bone in Northumbria, around 700. It is decorated with scenes from Christian stories and Anglo-Saxon legends. It was discovered in the nineteenth century being used as a work-box by a family in France.*

With busy trade came coins. The English progressed from the old barter system of simply exchanging goods, to the use of silver coins. The design of the silver penny which King Offa introduced was so good that it set the pattern for English coins until the fourteenth century.

Coins had to be the right weight to be of any value. In about 975, King Edgar 'ordered a new coinage to be made throughout England, because the old was so debased by the crime of clippers [who cut pieces from coins for their silver] that a penny hardly weighed a half-penny on the scales'.

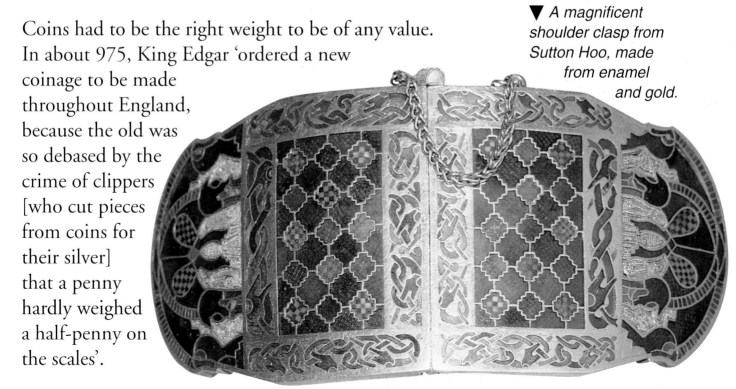

▼ *A magnificent shoulder clasp from Sutton Hoo, made from enamel and gold.*

19

chapter six

WHAT WERE THE ANGLO-SAXONS' RELIGIOUS BELIEFS?

One noble said of the new Christian belief: 'Life is like the flight of a sparrow through the hall ... While the bird is in the hall it is not touched by the storm, but after a little calm it vanishes into the night again. We see life for a little time, but not what comes before or after. If the New Teaching brings better knowledge, we should follow it.'

Under the Romans, Britain had become Christian. But the Anglo-Saxons who arrived in Britain were pagans. They worshipped ancient, fierce gods, such as Woden, god of wisdom, and Thunor, the thunder god. Some place-names still use these gods' names, such as Wednesbury, meaning Woden's burh or fort; and Thunderfield, meaning Thunor's plain.

In 597, the Christian missionary St Augustine came to Kent, landing on the Isle of Thanet with about forty men. Augustine sent a message to King Aethelbert with 'great news'. He 'promised eternal joy in heaven to those who obeyed him'.

Aethelbert became the first Christian Anglo-Saxon king, and other monarchs followed his example.

◄ *The early Anglo-Saxons sometimes cremated, or burnt, their dead, putting the ashes in a pottery urn. This sixth-century urn was found in a cemetery in Lincolnshire.*

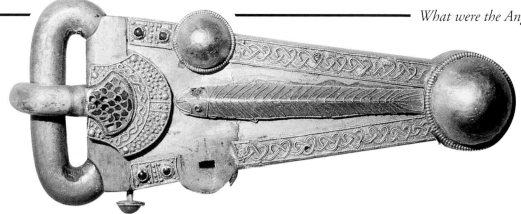

◀ *This gold and silver buckle found in Kent might suggest the Anglo-Saxons were becoming Christian. The fish in the centre is a Christian symbol.*

In 627, Edwin of Northumbria was baptized in York. He had vowed that he would become a Christian if he beat the West Saxons in battle. One of Edwin's priests had told him: 'Our old beliefs are useless. No-one was more meticulous than I in honouring the old gods, but others have received many more favours than I have.'

A king who became Christian might change his life. St Guthlac had led a war-band, burning and pillaging. An Anglo-Saxon poem tells us that Guthlac suddenly realized the 'shameful ends' of other kings of his family. He joined a monastery, then he became a hermit, living in a cave as a 'spiritual warrior'.

▼ *Some of our Anglo-Saxon heritage is hidden away, like St. Wystan's Church crypt in Derbyshire.*

One of the best records of these times was left by The Venerable Bede, a monk of Jarrow. In his *Ecclesiastical History* of 731, he writes: 'Such peace and prosperity reign in these days, that many of the Northumbrians ... take monastic vows rather than study the arts of war.'

Anglo-Saxons believed in monsters, demons, witches and magic cures. 'If a man is mad,' one cure says, 'take the skin of a porpoise, make a whip from it, and beat the mad man. He will soon be better.'

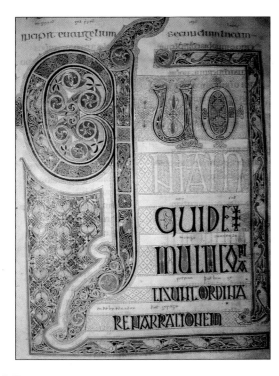

Monasteries and Books

This was a time when great monasteries were founded. In the mid-seventh century there were about twelve monasteries in Britain. A century later, there were at least 200.

St Benedict Biscop grew up at King Oswy's court in Northumbria. He became a monk and went on a twenty-year pilgrimage, returning to found monasteries in Monkwearwouth and Jarrow. These and other monasteries started to produce large numbers of religious books.

▲ *A page from the Lindisfarne Gospels shows the skill of the monks' illuminations.*

After books in Latin had been brought in by missionaries, writing became very popular. A book was a precious object, copied by hand and often beautifully 'illuminated' – decorated with amazingly detailed pictures and designs.

There were lives of saints, translations of the Bible, rules for monasteries and many books of law.

▶ *This illumination decorated a page of the* Codex Aureus, *a bible made at Canterbury in the eighth century.*

The monasteries grew rich. King Egfrith gave Monkwearmouth huge amounts of land. The Church could also claim a third of any treasure a king won at war. It collected taxes and fined those parents who did not baptize their children.

Monkwearmouth was wealthy enough to support nearly 700 monks. It paid for stone-masons from Gaul (France) to build a church boasting the first glass windows. The new monasteries were handsomely decorated with stone carvings. Some examples can still be seen today.

The old faith in magic survived within Christian beliefs. The feast of St John the Baptist included a burning of bones, a *bone-fire,* or bonfire as we would say. The idea was that: 'The dragons [that] so envenomed the waters and caused many deaths ... hate nothing more than the stench of brenning [burning] bones.' In some parts of Britain, bones were stored for bone-fires as late as 1800.

In a letter, St Cuthbert apologizes for a delay in book production: 'During the past winter, our island has been savagely oppressed with cold and ice and long storms, so that the scribes' hands became sluggish, and could not produce a large number of books.'

▼ The ruins of Lindisfarne monastery. Founded in 635, the monastery housed a library of books written by its monks.

chapter seven

WHAT WRITING DID THE ANGLO-SAXONS LEAVE US?

▲ *This silver object bears the runes that the Anglo-Saxons and Vikings both used as writing. It is probably a charm to keep off injury.*

The Anglo-Saxons had a great literature. Their stories, in long poems that were memorized, were their history too. The poets' memories were the Anglo-Saxons' 'library', until the introduction of writing around the seventh century.

The poet's job was to praise his leader for bravery in battle and generosity in giving gold. A good praise-poem was very valuable to both king and poet. When the poet Egill Skallagrimsson was due to be executed by King Eric Bloodaxe, Egill sang him a flattering poem. It saved his life.

The Anglo-Saxons wrote hundreds of riddles for their entertainment. Can you guess what this one describes?

One poet wrote about the Viking slaughter of English soldiers at Maldon: 'Here on the sand lies our leader, cut down. Those who leave the battle now will regret it forever. I am an old man, I will not leave, I intend to lie by my dear lord's side.'

> My nose is pointed downwards
> I crawl along and dig in the earth ...
> My guardian, at my tail, pushes his way on the plain,
> Lifts me and presses me on ...
> As I advance, on one side of me there is green,
> While on the other my black track is clear.

(The answer is on page 32.)

▲ *This Anglo-Saxon ivory carving shows a monk writing.*

Alfred

King Alfred was a great influence on Britain's literature. Asser says: 'By the carelessness of his parents and tutors, Alfred remained ignorant of letters till his twelfth year or even longer. But he listened attentively to Saxon poems day and night, and hearing them often recited by others committed them to memory.'

One law said that priests must run schools in their houses. But the priests had to learn too. Bishop Aldhelm wrote: 'The despair of doing sums oppressed my mind ... I grasped, after incessant study, the most difficult of all things, what they call fractions.'

Alfred believed that a ruler's duty was to promote wisdom. He says in the *Anglo-Saxon Chronicle* that he wishes 'all the youth in England born of free men to be devoted to learning until they can read English'. The *Chronicle* was mainly his idea.

One of Alfred's most important ideas was to translate Latin books into English. He was so keen that men should read and write that he ordered his judges to learn to read or give up their jobs.

▶ *A page from a gospel written in England shows St Matthew writing. It was found in Rheims, in France, and was probably a gift from Aelfgar, Earl of Mercia, whose son was buried there.*

chapter eight

WHAT HAPPENED
TO THE ANGLO-SAXONS?

When Aethelred became king in 979, the Vikings had started to raid England again with renewed fury. The English had no plan to defend themselves. Instead, they paid the Vikings gold – called *Danegeld* – to go away. Of course they came back, so as to be paid to go away again!

Finally the Vikings could no longer be paid off. The Danish Viking Swein became king of the Danelaw, and was succeeded by his son Cnut. When Aethelred died, Cnut attacked and captured London. He allowed Aethelred's son Edmund to rule as king of Wessex. When Edmund died, Cnut became the first Viking king of England.

▼ A silver penny minted at Chester or Shrewsbury, showing the head of King Cnut. It was about the same size as a modern penny. Sometimes pennies were cut up into halves and quarters, for change!

After Cnut's death there was a dispute about who should be king. One candidate, Alfred, was murdered on the orders of another, Harold, who himself was later poisoned. There followed a series of short reigns and rebellions. This struggle for the throne is a constant feature of British history. Finally, in 1066, Harold Godwinsson was chosen to be king.

William, Duke of Normandy, and Harald Hardrada, King of Norway, immediately invaded. King Harold defeated Hardrada in the north, then dashed south and was killed at the Battle of Hastings by William. William the Conqueror became the first Norman king of England.

So, Anglo-Saxon England came to an end with a typical Anglo-Saxon argument, over who should be king. The English had lost the argument and in some ways lost their country too. The richest nobles lost their land. By 1087, only one bishop in England was English. England was now ruled by French-speaking Normans, and by kings of England who could not speak English.

▼ *This picture from the* Bayeux Tapestry *created the legend that King Harold died after being shot in the eye with an arrow. Many historians now believe that Harold is the warrior being ridden down by the Norman horseman on the right.*

chapter nine

WHAT LEGACIES DID THE ANGLO-SAXONS LEAVE US?

Many places we live in or visit have Anglo-Saxon names. In Sussex, many place-names end with the Saxon 'ing', meaning 'people'. So, Steyning was for Stein's people. Other common Saxon endings are ham (home), head (hill), holt (thick wood), stoke (place or meeting place), ey (river), den (valley), ley (clearing). In the north are Gateshead, meaning goat's hill, and Dumfries, the fort of the Frisians.

Most of the shires into which Anglo-Saxon England was divided survive today. In Wessex, for instance, Hampshire, Wiltshire, Dorset and Somerset all existed by the ninth century.

Anglo-Saxon ideas for government survived for centuries, too, like the sheriff, the king's local agent and collector of fines and taxes. He remained important in England until about a hundred years ago.

▲ We can still sense the mystery and violence of the Anglo-Saxons' lives, through the objects that have been dug up from their graves.

Language

The English language is descended – through thirty or more generations of speakers – from Anglo-Saxon or Old English. There has been much change, but bits of Old English can be recognized. The Anglo-Saxon poem *The Seafarer* says of a sailor, *'he ne gehyrde butan hlimman sae'* – he heard nothing but the slam of the sea.

Thousands of the ordinary short words that we use all the time are from Old English. In *The Seafarer* can be found: hail, shower, flew, song, did, I, me, laughter, for, sing – all in forms close to their modern spellings.

▲ The thousands of brooches found in graves reveal the passion that the Anglo-Saxons had for brightly coloured jewellery.

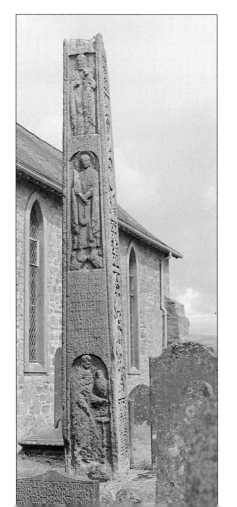

◄ *Bewcastle Cross in Cumbria is a typical Anglo-Saxon mixture of pagan and Christian. It is carved with images of Christ, runes commemorating the Northumbrian king Alcfrith, and various birds and beasts.*

Although England was under foreign control after 1066, there was by then such a thing as 'England', an English state. The *Anglo-Saxon Chronicle* tells us that after Alfred had taken London from the Danish, 'All the people submitted to him'. The idea of a united England grew from that time.

People could soon use the word 'England' and mean what we mean. So the main heritage of the Anglo-Saxons is quite simply – England.

GLOSSARY

Archaeologists People who study objects and remains from ancient times.

Brocade A rich fabric, often containing gold or silver thread.

Burh A fortified town.

British / Britons Tribes living in Britain before the Anglo-Saxons.

Churls Anglo-Saxon peasants who had to work for the lord of their land.

Clippers People who cut up coins for their silver.

Cobbler Someone who makes or mends shoes.

Coinage A system of minting and valuing coins.

Comet A bright object with a tail visible in the night sky, thought to be an omen.

Compensation Payment made to make up for an injury.

Consecrated Made sacred.

Cremated Burnt to ashes.

Danelaw The part of England ruled by the Danish Vikings from the ninth to the eleventh century.

Dyke A defensive embankment, especially of turf.

Feuding Continued arguments between two parties.

Fowler Someone who hunts or traps birds.

Grindstones Stones used for sharpening tools.

Hide A measure of land large enough to support one family.

Malt Barley or other grain dried for brewing.

Missionaries People who travel to a country to spread their religion.

Monasteries The buildings in which monks live.

Mosaics Pictures created from tiny fragments of coloured glass or stone.

Pagan Referring to people who are not Christians.

Picts Ancient tribes who raided from Scotland into Roman Britain.

Rebel To fight against your own government or rulers.

Smithy A blacksmith's workshop.

Thanes Anglo-Saxon nobles who were granted land by the king.

Vikings Scandinavian pirates and traders who raided and settled in Europe from the eighth to the eleventh century.

Weir An enclosure of stakes set in a stream to catch fish.

Yarn Thread which has been spun.

BOOKS TO READ

Tonge, Neil *History Detective Investigates: The Anglo-Saxons in Britain* (Wayland, 2006)

Savage, A (ed) *The Anglo-Saxon Chronicles* (Colour Library Books, 1996)

Hewitt, Sally *Starting History: The Anglo-Saxons* (Watts, 2006)

Liz Gogerly *Victorians: Reconstructed* (Wayland, 2005)

Williams, Brenda *Saxons and Vikings* (Pitkin Guides, 2001)

Wood, Tim *Saxons and Normans* (Ladybird, 1994)

PLACES TO VISIT

Sutton Hoo
Near Ipswich, Suffolk.
Site of the burial mound in which an Anglo-Saxon ship and treasures were found. Most of the treasures are now in the British Museum, London.

West Stow Anglo-Saxon Village
Near Bury St Edmunds, Suffolk.
A reconstruction of an Anglo-Saxon village, with houses built using tools of the time

Offa's Dyke
Knighton, Powys, Wales.
There is an information centre at one of the best parts of the dyke, in the village of Knighton.

There are Anglo-Saxon monasyeries and churches throughout Britian, including examples at Bradford-on-Avon, Wiltshire; Sompting, Sussex; Earls Barton, Northamptonshire; Lindisfarne, Northumberland; Jarrow, Tyne and Wear. There are remains of defences at burh towns such as Wareham, Dorset.

INDEX

Numbers in **bold** refer to pictures

Answer to the riddle on page 24: A plough.

Picture acknowledgements
The publishers would like to thank the following for permitting the reproduction of their pictures: Lesley and Roy Adkins Picture Library 10(bottom), 21(bottom), 23; Ancient Art and Architecture Collection 15; British Museum *cover*(left), 13(top); C.M.Dixon *cover*(right, bottom), 2, 3, 4(top), 5(top), 7, 9(right), 11, 12, 13(bottom), 14, 16-17, 18, 19, 20, 21(top), 22, 24, 25, 26, 28, 29; ET Archives 6; Robert Harding 4-5(bottom), 8-9(bottom); Michael Holford *cover*(centre), *title page*, 17(top); Reading Museum Service 27; Wayland Picture Library 10(top). The maps on pages 4 and 8 are by Peter Bull Design.